CompTIA CSA+. Exam Guide (Exam CS0-001)

Cybersecurity Analyst Certification

Table of Contents

Introduction

Cyber-attacks are on the rise. This can be attributed to the advancement in technology. Organizations are also in competition, each trying to outdo their competitors. This calls for organizations to protect their sensitive information so that it doesn't leak to their competitors. Organizations also need to keep on surveying their computer systems, especially the organization network so as to detect any attempts to intrude into the organization's systems. There is also a need for enterprises to stay prepared to respond effectively in case a cyber-attack occurs. This book helps you know all aspects of cybersecurity and how organizations can stay protected against cyber-attacks. You will also know how to respond effectively to cyber-attacks. Enjoy reading!

Chapter 1- Defending Against Cybersecurity Threats

The best way for us to stay protected today is by enriching the tools we use with threat intelligence, understanding the tools malicious hackers use and analyzing what may indicate that there is a threat. Signatures are used for detection of threat activities and alert the incidence response team. It is a cost-effective way through which we can deal with threats, but it requires us to possess the knowledge of the indicators. Threat actors are capable of adapting both manual and automated ways, which makes some of the common indicators to become irrelevant.

The security techniques implemented in any organization should be diversified. All the network endpoints should protect, and the employees should be aware of the various measures to ensure the organization is safe from cyber-attacks. The employees should also be trained regularly.

Identifying Cybersecurity Threats

As IT security experts are developing new security mechanisms, cyber criminals are inventing new ways on how to attack the organizations. Organizations should not just install the necessary security software, train the employees then relax.
They should stay updated about the latest cyber security threats so that they can thwart any attempts to attack their systems.

Below are the cyber threats which are facing organizations:

- Advanced Persistent Threats
- Trojans
- Phishing
- Botnets
- Distributed Denial of Service (DDoS)
- Ransomware
- Wiper Attacks
- Theft of Money
- Intellectual Property Theft
- Data Manipulation

- Spyware/Malware
- Data Destruction
- Man in the Middle (MITM)
- Malvertising
- Drive-By Downloads
- Unpatched Software
- Rogue Software

Other than identifying a cyber threat, it is good to know the individual or organization behind the threat. The following are some of the common sources of cyber threats:

- Nation states and national governments
- Industrial spies
- Terrorists
- Organized crime groups
- Business competitors
- Hacktivists and hackers
- Disgruntled insiders

The following are some of the ways through which we can identify the cybersecurity threats:

1.   Watch for spear phishing

This is a twist in phishing. It is an email which comes from a sender who appears to be well known by the recipient. Spear phishing attacks also target companies and individuals. These emails are geared towards soliciting for sensitive information from the recipient. The recipient may be persuaded to give out account numbers, usernames and passwords, which puts the security of the organization at risk.

Note that these details are not requested for directly, but the recipient is directed to a web form where they will fill in the details. Employees should be trained about spear phishing attacks, since no legitimate request will ask for usernames and passwords.

2. Be prepared for Ransomware

Ransomware gets installed into a computer after an individual clicks on a link send through email. The link installs the ransomware, which in turn encrypts the documents. In some cases, the organization is asked to pay some ransom so as to get back their documents back. Documents should be backed up. Backing up documents in the cloud is safer since the ransomware can't access such documents. The backup can also be done on a server with a strong firewall.

3. Scan for Altered Documents

Criminals who hack into companies may not need to steal data. They can modify the data without the company noticing. The criminals can use the altered data to manipulate the market, or ask for payment so as to fix it.

Checks for data integrity should be implemented in the organization, and backups should be done in the cloud or a separate network.

4. Limit Access to Wearable Technology

Wearable technology such as watches and fitness devices can act as access points for hackers. This is because they store personal information and emails, and they have a direct access to computers and laptops. If the devices store sensitive information, hackers may use it so as to hack into the workplace of the individual.

Networks should be required to prompt for username and password when one is connecting, thus, remote equipment won't be able to access the network continuously. Wearable devices without credentials won't be able to access the network.

5. Identify Social Media Data Leaks

Hackers in most scan social media to look for accounts which provide too much sensitive information. Such information may include the place of employment, the name of supervisors, addresses and screenshots for documents. If employees of an organization share too much information online, the organization is at risk of cyber-attacks.

Documents should be protected, and employees should be made aware of the risks of sharing such data on social media.

6. Monitor Online Payments

For companies which make online payments, they are at risk of cyber-attacks as hackers can steal sensitive information from them. Hackers will target customers will less sophisticated security mechanisms. The customer credentials can be used to access the payment department of the organization.

A security firewall should be implemented between the customer accounts and the company's financial data and payroll.

7. Malware in the Cloud

Companies doing cloud computing are expected to be infected by malware. Such malware can compromise data, interrupt computing, render apps useless and destroy the IT infrastructure. The solution is to back up could data in on storage devices such as servers located on the premises of the organization.

8. Avoid Mal-advertising

Some sites have ads which are placed by hackers. Such ads may have malware. If your organization's employees interact with such ads, the malware will infect your computers.

The solution is to avoid clicking any ads displayed on websites, even though the site could be approved by the company. Employees should report any mishaps.

9. Explore vulnerabilities with open source software

The open source software you use in your organization may have vulnerabilities which can be an opportunity for hackers. Hackers are constantly looking for security loopholes in popular open source software, so it will be good for you to ensure you are protected against such. This requires constant monitoring. Use software which tries to hack into your open source software, and close any loopholes which might be identified.

Securing the Company Network

For a company or organization to stay secure from cyber-attacks, its network must be secured. It is through a secure network that a company will achieve integrity, confidentiality and availability of information. The following are some of the ways through which one can build a secure network for an institution:

1. Build a firewall

A firewall is one of the greatest ways of securing a computer network. The firewall will serve as a border control defining your perimeter. It will thwart any unauthorized attempts to access your network, even if the attempts are coming from the inside of the network. A firewall is not 100% way of protecting your network, but it is a great tool for thwarting cyber-attacks.

2. Use Secure Socket Layer (SSL)

This is a protocol which establishes security between a website (client) and web browser (server). It acts like a tunnel ensuring that information travelling between the server and the client is not accessed by unauthorized parties. This way, confidential information will remain private when it is under transmission. To stay safe, use this protocol to encrypt your connections.

3. Network Access Control (NAC)

Are you aware of what or who is accessing your network? If you are not, then you are just relying on assumption that your network is safe. During the early days of networks, where we had only wired connections, it was easy for one to identify and manage the devices connecting to their network. However, today with the Internet of Things (IoT) and the increasing number of mobile devices which are connecting to networks, the control of devices connecting to the network has become complex and more important. With Network Access Control, you are able to control the access to your network. It helps you to identify who, where, what, how and when a device or end-user is connecting to the network.

After a NAC system has identified all the above factors, it can assign roles to the devices/end-users or to the groups of the devices/end-users. The roles assigned will determine what one can do or access on the network and this process is known as "role-based access control". For example, if the role of the end-user or device is a student, they will be able to access learning applications, the internet and other internal resources needed by a student. If the access role is a guest, they should not be granted access to the internal applications of the company, but they should only be granted access to the internet and social media tools such as YouTube. Instagram etc.

4. Network Segmentation

In this technique, the network is subdivided into various subnetworks, with subnetwork forming a network segment. Most networks are protected through a strongly configured firewall. They also feature strong Intrusion Detection Systems (IDS) as well as strong Intrusion Prevention Systems (IPS). These keep on monitoring the network, making it for anyone to attack it.

However, an attacker may gain access to the network using strong mechanisms to evade these. If this happens, the attacker will find some flat network infrastructure. The Detection tools are more focused on the external network, but they forget what is happening on the inner part of the network. The attacker will have a free environment to perpetrate the attack. Although a flat network is easy to manage, malicious activities are more likely to happen in such a network.

With network segmentation, it becomes hard for an attacker to perpetrate an attack through your entire network. It is also a good technique for internal security as sensitive information can be isolated from the users.

In a flat network, all the workstation and servers are located on the same LAN. These systems do not have to talk to each other, or trust each other, so there is no need to put them together. If you allow them to communicate, you will have given an attacker with the opportunity to perpetrate an attack from one system to another. Segmentation can be done either virtually or physically. The result will be similar. Your goal is to limit communication between the network devices, and if an attacker can't communicate with it, they can't attack it.

Secure Endpoint Management

The endpoint devices, such as laptops, mobile devices and desktops should be protected. Security configurations should be implemented in these end-systems. The browsing process should be done securely. Their hard disks also need to be encrypted.

The security configurations on these systems should hardened as a way of ensuring they are secure. Even though you have configured a strong security mechanism, you have to maintain the configurations as a way of ensuring they are not compromised.

These devices should also be scanned continuously for the purpose of identifying any vulnerability. Any flaws identified should be addressed immediately so that attackers don't take advantage of them and attack your systems.

The organization should come up with group policies that will help ensure the organization remains secure from cyber-attacks.
Each member of the group should adhere to these policies. Any employee who violates the policies should be punished so that other members can take them seriously.

Penetration Tests

An organization should analyze its Information technology systems so as to identify their weak points. This will give the organization insights to know what is required for it to remain protected against cyber-attacks. It also helps organizations assess various security systems and identify the best ones for their security. This is done through penetration testing.

With penetration testers, an organization can assess the security of its systems and come up with a prioritized view of what should be done so as to stay protected. Once the gaps in security systems of the organization are established, the penetration testers can give the organization recommendations on how to close them.

Some organizations have their own experts who can do penetration testing. Other organizations do not have such, so they have to seek the services of a penetration testing provider.

The tester should enumerate the target network so as to determine the vulnerable accounts or systems. Each system should be scanned for the open ports which might have services running on them.

It is rare to have a network which has been configured properly and passwords which have been protected properly and fully patched. The penetration tester should have a good understanding of the organization's network, and then use a penetration testing tool so as to try to exploit any available vulnerability.

A penetration tester in most cases will target the users of the network via pre-text calling, phishing emails and onsite social engineering.

Preparing and Executing a Penetration Test

The following are some of the tips which can help prepare and execute a penetration test:

1. Execute regular vulnerability scans
Scanning and remediation should be done on a monthly basis, with an aim of fixing both the high and medium vulnerabilities. This is a good technique to keep you prepared for the annual penetration testing.

2. Patch software regularly
You should include all your third party software. The Adobe products especially the Flash present a vulnerability to a system. In case you only patch the operating system only, then you are leaving too much vulnerability in your system.
3. Minimize the local administrator privileges
Malwares usually run in regards to the security context of the user who is logged in, that is, they exploit the privileges accorded to that user within the system. In case there are some applications which need some special privileges so as to run, use the "Run As" command to run them or run them using the "Compatibility Mode".

4. Configure the systems securely
All systems should have the Link-Local Multicast Name Resolution (LLMNR) and NetBIOS disabled. These are old broadcast protocols which are developed for back-up compatibility. When these are disabled, the attack surface will be greatly reduced. All legacy

systems running on the network should be inspected as a way of ensuring that the protocols are not required.

You should also require SMB signing. With this, the servers on the network can have communications between themselves which are digitally signed. Unauthorized devices and servers will not be able to communicate with these.

5. Passwords
Use Microsoft Local Administrator Password Solution (LAPS) as a way of ensuring each device has a unique local administrator password. Password policies should also be implemented stating the complexity and length of passwords, and use technical controls to ensure that these are adhered to.
Default passwords should also be changed for all applications. You should also use password managers for a secure password management.

Reverse Engineering

This refers to the process of taking something part then putting it back together so as to see the way it works. With reverse engineering, one can identify any security flaws in software. Some companies also use this technique so as to protect themselves against such security flaws. Reverse engineering helps greatly in malware analysis. With this, the organization can understand how the parts of the malware function.

After the analysis of the malware, organizations should come with a well-organized incidence response mechanism. They can also create signatures which will help them stay protected against the malware. Organizations can also track and get to the criminals who created the malware. There are various software tools which can be used in an organization for reverse engineering.

Isolation and Sandboxing

Sandboxing is simply a process used for detection of malicious software according to their behavior as opposed to their signature.

The purpose of sandboxing systems is to watch the systems and networks for any unknown pieces of code, and if an application which has never been seen before is detected, it is isolated into some special environment which is known as a *sandbox*. This application will not be able to access the organization systems while in the sandbox. The application will then be executed from the sandbox so as to observe its behavior. If the application is found to show a strange behavior, it is blocked from entering the network. The application may be meant to scan the network and collect sensitive information, which is a cyber-threat.

Detecting and Preventing Reconnaissance

Reconnaissance attacks normally begin with an attack on the network from an infected endpoint so as to locate the assets and services which an attacker needs to target. Most reconnaissance includes random, active IP and stealth scanning.

There are tools which can be used to detection any kind of detection from an attacker. Attivo is one of such tools. The tool uses deception-based threat detection solutions so as to identify all types of scanning.

As a way of staying protected against reconnaissance, you can scan your own network. Schedule regular vulnerability scans and asset identification then prioritize vulnerability patching.

Chapter 2- Reconnaissance and Intelligence Gathering

When a security professional is in need of knowing the security levels in an organization, they must begin by gathering information.

Foot printing

This is a process of gathering information about a computer system. The goal in foot printing is to gather as much information as possible regarding a system. This information can include its ability to access remote systems, its services and ports as well as its security aspects. It is through foot printing that you are able to identify the weaknesses or vulnerabilities of a system such bas a network system.

A person's digital footprint refers to the data they leave behind when they are using a digital service. The following are the two types of footprints:

1. Active digital footprint
This is created when persons share information online such as when they are sending an email, signing up for some newsletter, publishing a blog or during posting of content on social media.

2. Passive digital footprint
This refers to the data which is collected by search engines when they are storing the search history of a person, when web servers are logging the IP address of their computer and when they visit a website, or when smartphones are tracking their location.

You may not actively engage yourself in online activities, but others will expose you but sharing your photos or information.

There are various tools such as scanning engines which can provide you with a means to search your systems and identify any weak points. Any misconfigurations and potential vulnerabilities can also be identified in the process.

DNS Foot printing

With DNS foot printing, one is able to enumerate the details of DNS records and the type of servers. The following are the various DNS records which can provide us with information regarding the target location:

- A/AAAA
- NS
- SVR
- TXT
- CNAME
- MX
- SOA
- PTR
- RP
- HINFO

Domain dossier is one of the online tools which can be used for the purpose of DNS foot printing as well as whois foot printing.

Whois Lookup

This is commonly used when one is querying the databases which are storing the list of the registered users or the assignees of a particular internet resource like an IP address block, a domain name or autonomous system, but there is a wider range of information for which this can be used. The protocol is capable of storing and delivering the contents of the database in a format which is readable. Some of the tools which can be used for whois foot printing include Caller IP, Whois lookup multiple address, Whois Analyzer pro.

Port Scanning

Ports can be scanned to give a lot of information. There are several port scanning techniques, and one has to choose one depending on the amount of time they want to spend doing the test.
If you have zero knowledge about the organization systems, you can do a fast ping scan so as to identify the systems. To detect the common ports which are available, you can run a quick scan with no ping verification, that is, -PN in nmap. After this comes to an end, we can run a more comprehensive scan. Most people check only for the open TCP ports, but it is good for one to check even the UDP ports.

Banner Grabbing

This is an enumeration technique used to gather information about the computer systems of a network and the services which are running on the ports. With banner grabbing, one can tell the operating system that a host is running and the versions of applications which are running on the system.

Banner grabbing is normally done on Hyper Text Transfer Protocol (HTTP), Simple Mail Transfer Protocol (SMTP), and File Transfer Protocol (FTP) on the ports 80, 25 and 21 respectively. The common tools used to do banner grabbing include telnet, Netcat and nmap.

Prevention against Reconnaissance

For us to prevent reconnaissance from being done on our network, we can use a combination of Intrusion Detection Systems (IDS)/Intrusion Prevention Systems (IPS) and a firewall.
These will notify us of any active reconnaissance attacks. They can be blocked or one decides not to access certain subnets or services so as to prevent launching of attacks such as DoS floods and buffer overflow attacks.

Unauthorized reconnaissance can also be prevented by disabling the unused services which can be used for the purpose of gathering information about target systems and the intermediate network devices which are protecting them. A strong encryption is also essential for us to prevent unauthorized access and reconnaissance attacks.

Chapter 3- Designing a Vulnerability Management Program

The increase in cyber-crime is making most organizations focus on more on information security. A vulnerability management program can help the organization control the information security risks. With such a program, the organization is capable of continuously getting a view of the vulnerabilities in their environment d the risks which are associated with them. When vulnerabilities are detected and mitigated, the opportunity for the hackers to penetrate into an organization's network and steal information will be reduced.

With the evaluation, the vulnerabilities can be corrected and removing the risk or formal risk acceptance by the top management in the organization.

Scanning for Vulnerabilities

This is the process of using a computer program to identify the vulnerabilities in a computer network, applications or computer infrastructure. The vulnerability management is the process which surrounds vulnerability scanning, and it takes into account factors such as remediation, risk acceptance etc.

Scoping Vulnerability Scans

One has to determine what will be scanned during the vulnerability scan. If you need your scan to cover only the in-scope systems, networks and process, you have to specify this. If you fail to specify the scope of what is to be scanned, your scan might overlook some of the important networks.

However, for organizations relying on a flat network, you don't have to worry about this problem. Such networks are not segmented, meaning that the whole of the network should be scanned. For the case of complex networks which take advantage of segmentation so as to regulate the scope should consider how the scope changes in a year, and the vulnerability scans should be adjusted accordingly. It is recommended that you perform a scan whenever there is a change in the network configuration.

Remediating Vulnerabilities

This involves evaluation of the vulnerabilities which have been identified assigning risk to the vulnerabilities, planning the responses to these vulnerabilities and tracking any actions which are taken towards the vulnerabilities which are found. If vulnerabilities are found, the organization needs to do something about them. If the organization fails to do this, they will be exposed to a great risk.

Patching Vulnerabilities

The following are some of the ways through which vulnerability and patch management can be done:

First, one must use tools and processes to identify all the available vulnerabilities. These should also be set to help in identifying any confirmed or suspected threats in the organization.

The findings should then be analyzed thoroughly so that we can understand the risks better. It is impossible for you to implement the correct measure if you don't have the correct understanding of the risk.

Once you have done the analysis, you can fix the problem. After the fix has been implemented, you must test it to ensure that it was fixed correctly.

Dealing with Barriers

Although vulnerability scanning is very essential for the organization to remain safe from cyber-attacks, organization's employees in other departments other than the IT department may not see its importance. The cybersecurity experts should be aware of these barriers and come up with effective ways to deal with them. They must overcome barriers including the following:
1. Customer commitments
These may be a barrier to vulnerability scanning. If the scan may affect how services are provided to customers, then allow the customers to take part in the decision making process. Come up with service level agreements (SLAs) and memorandums of understandings.

2. Service degradations
During vulnerability scans, a lot of bandwidth is consumed. The applications and customers are also not able to utilize the systems which are being scanned. Even if they might be allowed to use them, the performance of the system may be degraded. This can lead to

service disruptions. To avoid this, cybersecurity professionals should tune how the bandwidth is consumed and come with schedules for performing the scans.

3. IT governance rules and change management
A lot of bureaucracy may be involved to make the necessary configurations for scanning to be done. The cybersecurity experts should adhere to these when getting the resources necessary for the vulnerability scan to be done.

Chapter 4- Analysing Vulnerability Scans

Once a vulnerability scan is done, reports are generated. These reports need to be analyzed by security professionals. It is through this the false reports can be identified. The steps to be taken so as to remediate should also be prioritized and the root cause of the problem identified.

Analysing the Scan Reports

A vulnerability report gives too much information about the vulnerabilities which are identified in detail. The details of the report can be imported into a spreadsheet, SQL files etc. It is from this one can perform sorting on the items.

When the report items are exported into a spreadsheet, it becomes easy for the analyst to sort and run queries on the items. This way, you should be able to deal with a single vulnerability at a time across a number of hosts.

Identifying False Positives

Now that you have presented the results into a format which you can understand easily, you can begin to analyze them while proposing solutions to the problems.

Sometimes, the tool that you use for scanning may get it wrong. If we use appropriate techniques are used, the level of accuracy can be increased, but it is good for a human to make the final judgment. Due to the use of many software and the configurations used, the results obtained can be confusing.

Common Vulnerabilities

The following are the common types of vulnerabilities:

1. Network vulnerabilities

All network devices should be accessed to identify vulnerabilities. Applications, operating systems, services and ports should be scanned against and updated in the vulnerability database.

Operating systems and the software running on the networking devices should be updated regularly. If not, these will be vulnerability.

The network may also have TLS (Transport Layer Security) and SSL (Secure Sockets Layer) which are outdated, and this is vulnerability. These two protocols are used to ensure there is a secure communication on a network.

If some of the ciphers are prone to eavesdropping attacks, they will be identified as vulnerability. Certificates and signatures used for exchange of information over a network may have a problem such as a mismatch, which is also vulnerability.

2. Web Applications Vulnerability
Web applications are many up of many components including backend-databases, servers and other systems which facilitate the provision of services to the end-users. These components may have some security weaknesses which can be exploited by cyber criminals.

During the vulnerability scan, the cybersecurity experts may identify vulnerability for injection attacks, which normally allow the attackers to evade the common procedure of accessing the backend services, but they access the backend services directly.

Websites may also be prone or vulnerable to cross-scripting attacks (XSS), in which an attacker attaches some scripts on a website which will be run later when an unsuspecting user visits the website. Note the user is genuine and he or she is trying to access a genuine website, unknowing that an attacker has attached a malicious script for them to execute.

3. Database Vulnerability

Each organization uses a database management system such as MySQL, Oracle, and Microsoft SQL Server etc. During a vulnerability scan, the cybersecurity experts may find that the database is prone to attacks such as SQL injection attacks. Note that users are not normally granted a direct access to an organization's database. However, cyber-criminals may use mechanisms to gain a direct access into the database. These can be identified during the vulnerability scan.

4. Virtual Vulnerability
There are vulnerabilities associated with applications which run on virtual environments such as VMware. In datacenter environments, the virtual machine runs on a host operating system, commonly referred to as the "hypervisor".

An example of a vulnerability associated with virtualization is the virtual machine escape. In this case, an attacker who gains access to a single virtual machine can take advantage of this to gain access and perform a malicious activity on the resources assigned for use by another virtual machine. It is the work of the hypervisor to ensure that the virtual machine can only access the resources assigned to it. If this logic is not implemented, it is vulnerability.

If the virtual machine is not updated, this is vulnerability. This is because when virtual machines are updated, they stay protected from latest forms of attacks. During the configuration of the virtual environment, the management interface is normally used. If this interface is found not to be well secured during the vulnerability scan process, it will be treated as vulnerability. It is the work of the cybersecurity experts to ensure that this interface cannot be accessed directly from a public network. The virtual machines which run on the same network may also communicate, even on the hard disk level. If one is running multiple virtual machines from a single host, each should be treated in the form of an independent operating system.

Chapter 5- Building an Incident Response Program

Organizations should be prepared to handle any cybersecurity incidence in case it occurs. Cyber-criminals are constantly evolving their techniques, so you need to stay updated by using the latest security patches. However, note that a cyber-criminal only needs to identify single weaknesses in your organization's systems so as to exploit it. It is good for each organization to be adequately prepared so as to respond well to any incidences of a cyber-attack.

Incident Response Tips

For you to minimize the impact of a cyber-attack, your organization should prepare a plan early in advance. When developing this plan, the following are the necessary tips for you to consider:

1. Be ready for the worst
You should not wait for a cyber-attack to occur so that you can build an incident response program. Security should be implementing as an investment for the organization. You should come up with an adequate budget and determine the resources which will be used to respond to a cyber-attack. These should then be followed in any case an attack occurs. All the company stakeholders should be involved when coming up with the plan. Proper protocols should be laid down so that an irreversible damage may not occur during an attack, but action will be taken early enough.

2. Consider the little things
Other than focusing on the big picture, consider the small things too. It is always too hard for one to stay too organized when it comes to security, and cybersecurity is not different. Identify the key tasks, determine the timelines and write down all the efforts right from the start to the end so as to know where some refinement is needed. Threats are constantly improving, so don't assume that your response plan is perfect.

3. Every effort counts

If a security breach occurs, it becomes hard for an organization to implement the security tools. Organizations are advised to invest in security right from the start to the end so as to make the process economical. This should be the cases for organizations with scarce human and financial resources.

4. Involve everyone
All the employees in your organization should be ready and involved in a security response program. Every employee should also be educated on the best cybersecurity responses so that incidences of cyber-attacks can be minimized.

Incident Response Stages

For a cyber-attack incident, an effective approach should be followed so as to counter it. The teams must follow an organized and coordinated approach. The following are the steps which an organization should follow when responding to a cyber-attack:

1. Preparation
Preparation is very essential for an effective incident response. Without a set of predetermined guidelines, it will be hard for a response team to do their work effectively. The incidence response plan should define the necessary incident response policies as well as the associated procedures and agreements. Communication guidelines should also be created so as to ensure a proper communication during and after the incident. The incident response team should conduct exercise which will help them know the incidents which are happening in the environment. You should also assess your ability to respond to events and make any necessary improvements.

2. Detection and Reporting
In this step, the incident response team has to monitor the security events so as detect, alert then report any potential security incidences.The monitoring of the security events is done using intrusion prevention systems, firewalls and data loss prevention.

3. Containment and Neutralization
This is a very critical stage in an incident response process. The strategy used for containment and neutralization of the threats is determined by the intelligence and the gathered which was gathered during the analysis phase. Once the security is verified and the system restored, the normal operations can be resumed.

A coordinated shutdown may be needed once all the systems which have been compromised by the threat actor are identified. All these systems are shut down, and notifications must be sending to the incident response team members so as to ensure there is a coordinated timing.

The infected devices can be wiped and the operating system rebuild from ground up. Passwords for all the compromised accounts should be changed.

In case you identify IP addresses and domains which come from threat actors, give threat mitigation requests for communications from these to be blocked.

4. Post-Incident Tasks
Once the issue has been solved, there is still much to be done. If you identify any information which can be used for mitigation of similar attacks in the future, just document them. The incident should be documented well so that the incident response plan can be improved and take any security measures for prevention of such incidents from occurring in the future.

Even after the incident, you should continue monitoring the activities since the threat actors will appear again. You can use a security log and hawk through it to analyze the data and check whether there are signs of any attack on your systems. New measures also need to be created so as to prevent any attacks in the future.

The Incident Response Team

This is the team which will be responding to security breaches, especially the cyber-attacks. The team should include technical experts and specialists who can guide the organization supervisors on how to implement a proper communication in the case of a cyber-attack. At the core, the incident response team should be made of the following members:

1. Incident Response Manager
He is responsible for overseeing and prioritizing actions during detection, analysis and the containment of the incident. The Incident Response Manager is also responsible for communicating the special requirements of the high severity incidents to the company members.

2. Security Analysts

The manger works together with a team of security analysts who work directly with the network so as to find the location, time and other details in case a network attack incident occurs. The following are the various types of analysts:

• Triage Analysts- these are responsible for filtering our false positives and watching for potential intrusions.

• Forensic Analysts- these are responsible for recovering key artifacts and maintaining the integrity of evidence so as to ensure there is a forensically sound investigation.

3. Threat Researchers

These provide threat intelligence and context for the incident so as to compliment the efforts of the security analysts. They constantly combine the internet and identify intelligence which might have been reported externally. When this information is combined with the company records regarding the previous incidences, a database of internal intelligence can be building and maintained.

Chapter 6- Analysing Symptoms for Incident Response

Organizations should continually monitor their networks for any unexpected devices, high bandwidth consumption or any other unusual behavior in the network. This is because these are always an indication of a cyber-attack. Cybersecurity experts should use the necessary tools so as to analyze these on an organization's network.

Router-Based Network Monitoring

Cybersecurity professionals can rely on the routers used on a network for the purpose of monitoring the trend of the traffic flowing on the routers. Attackers may sometimes disable the network device, but with this type of monitoring, the cybersecurity professionals can know its status. Other than routers, one can also use switches with routing capabilities.

All the devices which connect to a network must do so through a router. This provides us with a single point where data transfers and bandwidth usage can be monitored and even logged. However, this is not easy. Most routers don't know the amount of bandwidth being used by any of the connected devices, or even the amount of data they might have downloaded.

This calls for us to use some third-party router firmware. With router firmware such as DD-WRT, we are able to see live bandwidth usage, and you are able to see the devices which are using most data. This way, you are able to pinpoint the devices which may be hogging the network bandwidth.

Examples of tools which can be used to capture flows as well as other router information include RMON, Netflow and SNMP (Simple Network Management Protocol).

Network Monitoring and Analysis Tools

There are various tools which can be used for monitoring services, devices, ports and protocols as well as analyzing the traffic flowing on the network. These include the following:

1. Nagios

This is a network monitoring tool which can help one ensure that their critical applications, systems and services run continuously. Some of its common features include alerting, reporting and event handling. The Nagios Core is the main part of the tool since it provides a basic web UI and a core monitoring engine. On top of this core, you are able to add plugins which can help you in monitoring services, metrics and applications. One can also add add-ons for load distribution, graphs, data visualization, MySQL database support and others.

Install the tool and begin to use it for monitoring your services and hosts, and you will be able to tell the status of your systems.

2. Advanced IP Scanner

This is a tool which can be used to detect any devices on a network. The device is fast and easy to use, and it can detect even WIFI devices like printers, mobile phones and WIFI routers. It allows you to connect to common devices like FTP, HTTP and shared folders if they have been enabled on a remote machine. The tool can also be used for starting and shutting down remote machines.

3. Splunk

This is data collection and analysis tool which allows one to gather, monitor and analyze data from different sources on a network. One can setup alerts which will notify them whenever something goes wrong, or use the extension search provided by Splunk. The system also allows you to install applications which will allow you to extend its functionality.

After installing and logging into Splunk for the first time, add the data source and configure the indexes so as to get started. After doing that, you will be able to build dashboards, create reports and search so as to analyze data.

4. NetworkMiner

This tool captures the network packets then parses data so as to extract images and files, making it easy for you to reconstruct events which a user has taken on the network. This can also be done by parsing some pre-captured PCAP file. It is possible for you to enter the keywords which will be highlighted during the capture of the network packets. The tool is classified as a NFAT (Network Forensic and Analysis Tool) which can get information like hostname, open ports and the operating system from the host.

After loading the tool, choose the network adapter which you need to bind to then click the "Start" button and the packet capture process will be initiated.

Common Network Issues

Cybersecurity professionals should use monitoring tools so as to detect some of the common problems with networks. These problems are always an indication of a cyber-attack. The following are some of the issues which need to be detected:

1. Failed links

Physical links on a network may fail, and this may disrupt communication over a network. Both the hardware and firmware used in the network may fail. Link failures should be detected as quickly as possible so that they can be repaired and provision of services to users resume to normal.

When monitoring traffic, if the flow stops instantly, this can be an indication of a failed link. There are several ways for you to detect failed links, including the use of syslog events and SNMP monitoring.

2. Increased bandwidth consumption

An increase in the use of bandwidth may mean that certain network nodes will not have bandwidth for transmission of the data over the network. This can lead to service disruptions. In most networks, the data is send to a central system so that it can in turn provide alerts as far as bandwidth consumption is concerned.

Most network monitoring tools are set to a certain threshold, so that when the bandwidth usage reaches or exceeds this threshold, an alarm is raised. Examples of tools which can be used to monitor network bandwidth usage include SNMP and PRTG.

3. Beaconing
It may happen that some stations on the network do not receive transmissions. With beaconing, a station on a network can notify the other stations whenever it is not receiving transmissions. The cause of this might be a cyber-attack, so detecting this will help the cybersecurity professionals to take an immediate action. Beaconing is mostly applied in FDDI and Token Ring networks.

With beaconing, networks are able to render problems by themselves. It is also used in wireless networks to send signals in cases of problems. When a failure occurs, the packets are transmitted in the form of packets. The beacon is able to identify the configuration used in the neighboring node, and then apply it to the affected node so that it can bypass the failure.

How to detect and handle various Network Attacks

For you to be able to detect the various attacks on a network, you should first determine the characteristics which are associated with them. Let us discuss the various ways of detecting and handling the various types of attacks:

1. Denial-of-Service and Distributed Denial of Service Attacks
The purpose of a denial of service attack is to prevent access to a particular network resource such as a network printer. A good characteristic of this type of attack is sending of too many requests to the resource so that it can be overwhelmed. Consistent attacks on a particular network resource so as to make it fail may also be an indication of a denial-of-service attack. A resource or a system working between two systems may also be attacked so that the two systems do not communicate.

If the attacks are originating from a single source, the source should be blocked. There are various ways to do this, such as by use of a network firewall. The source will not be able to access the network. Organizations should implement intrusion prevention systems (IPS) on their network so as to prevent such attacks from occurring.

In distributed denial of service attacks, the attacks normally originate from multiple sources. Detecting these types of attacks may be attack since they originate from multiple sources. To detect these types of attacks, cybersecurity professionals can use IDS and IPS systems. These should have the options for detecting DOS and DDOS attacks enabled.

2. Scans
Scans are normally carried out on a network before an attack on the network is launched. Network scans can be identified or detected based on their characteristics. Connections to multiple IP addresses on a network are an indication of a network scan. Also, a potential attacker may also send continuous requests to network services which are not active.

To detect network scans, cybersecurity specialists can use firewalls as well as IDS and IPS systems.
3. Malicious hardware
Cyber-criminals can build cheap hardware devices which can be used to breach networks and capture very sensitive data. Malicious or rogue device are built with an intention of perpetrating a malicious activity such as capturing passwords, debit and credit card numbers, keystrokes, pins and proprietary or confidential information. There are various tools which have been specifically designed and developed for detection of such devices on a network. A good example is the pulse analytics tool.

Chapter 7- Forensic Analysis

Computer forensics refers to the application of investigation and analysis techniques so as to gather and preserve evidence from a certain computing device in such a way that it can be used as evidence especially in a court of law. In computer forensics, a structured investigation is carried out and a documented chain of evidence is maintained so as to know what happened on the computing device and the individual behind it.

How to Build a Forensic Toolkit

It is always good for any organization to build their own digital evidence collection toolkit. To build this, you need some equipment as well as supporting items which include forms, office supplies and documentation tools. Once you get all the tools, you will be ready to build your own forensic toolkit.

However, the type of tools you need to build a forensic toolkit will depend on the needs of your organization.

Steps in a Forensic Investigation

Cybersecurity experts must go through a number of steps when carrying out a forensic investigation. These steps include the following:

1. Verification
The computer forensics investigation is normally done as part of incident response scenario, meaning that the first step should be to verify whether the incident happened. The scope and breadth of the incident should also be investigated. With the necessary information, the experts will know the best steps to be taken so as to collect the evidence.

2. System Description
In this step, you gather data regarding the incident. You describe the system that you need to analyze, and the role the system plays in both the network and the organization. Determine the type of the

operating system and its configuration, the amount of RAM, disk format and location of the evidence.

3. Evidence Acquisition
Determine the data sources, acquire both volatile and non-volatile data, and then verify the integrity of this data. Volatile data changes from time to time, it is good for you to consider the order you use to collect the data. The collection of data should be collected from trusted binaries instead of doing it from the impacted system. Once you have collected volatile data, you can begin to collect the non-volatile data from the hard disk. Volatile data can be collected from ARP cache, network connections, running processes, login sessions, RAM contents and open files. To collect data from a hard disk, you can use a hardware device such as write blocker if it is possible for you to put the hard disk offline or make it to be accessible remotely only. Once you have acquired the data, you must verify its integrity.

4. Time Analysis
Once you have acquired the evidence, you should begin to do the analysis and investigation in a forensic lab. You should begin with a time analysis. You can get information about when files where modified, accessed and changed. They can then be changed to a human-readable format called MAC time evidence. A number of tools are used to gather the data and it is extracted from metadata layer of file system. It is then parsed and sorted before being analyzed. At the end, a snapshot should be generated and this should state the date, action, the artifact involved and the source.

5. Media and Artifact Analysis
At this point, you should know the programs that were executed, the files that were downloaded, the files clicked, the directories opened, the files deleted, where the user browsed etc. At this step, you may be overwhelmed by the amount of data that you may have. To reduce the amount of data, you can identify both the good and the bad files. This can be done using databases such as Nation Software Reference Library from the NIST. You can also do hash comparisons with tools such as hfind from Sleuth Kit. For those analyzing a Windows timeline, it is possible for you to create a super timeline.

This is capable of incorporating many time sources into one file. You can also look for evidence of browser usage, account usage, file opening/creation, file downloads, usb key usage and program execution. You can also analyze the memory so as to examine network connections, rogue processes, code injection evidence, loaded DLLs, mutex, user handles, process paths and others.

6. String/Byte Search

This is the step where the low level raw images are searched. If you are aware of what you need to find, then use this tool. You use tools and techniques which will find byte signatures of files called magic cookies. It is also the step you do string searches by use of regular expressions. The byte signatures or strings you are looking for are the ones which are significant to what you are dealing with.

7. Data Recovery

This is the step for recovering data from the file system. You should use tools capable of analyzing the data layer, file system and metadata layer. Examples of such tools are the ones provided in the Sleuth Kit. Files of interest can be found by analyzing the file system, unallocated space and the slack pace. You can carve files from raw images depending on the file headers for a further gathering of evidence.

8. Reporting Results

Now that you have performed the analysis, this is the step in which you should report the results you have obtained. The report may include the actions you have performed, the actions which need to be done and recommendations on improvements to be made on guidelines, procedures, policies, tools as well as other aspects of the forensic process. Reporting is a very essential step in a forensic investigation. The report should be written in a scientific manner with facts which can be proved. The reporting style chosen should be based on the audience and whether the evidence is to be presented in a court of law or not.

Chapter 8- Identity and Access Management

With identity and access management, an organization will be able to determine users who are authorized to access the organization's systems and those who are not supposed to. The organization can also grant different access rights which will determine what various users are allowed to do in the systems.

Context-Based Authentication

This type of authentication establishes a balance between trust and risk by allowing one to implement simple policies which can allow or deny access to web applications depending on contextual information like group membership, user role, location/IP address, device usage and geographical location.

This type of authentication is able to adapt to context changes dynamically in order to:

• Restrict access to the high-risk applications with sensitive data to specific IP addresses and or known office locations.

• Limit access of applications to trusted or approved devices.

• Prompt users to authenticate using a 2-factor authentication (2FA) to access particular applications.

The following are the features and benefits which you consider when choosing a context-based authentication:

1. Single sign-ons
An IT security solution should be convenient to the users. The Single sign-on systems are developed to provide the authorized users with a frictionless and secure access to the critical applications from some single login point.

Context-based authentication achieves this by combining identity analytics, device analytics and login context so as to determine whether an attempt to login a system comes from an authentic BYOD user.

2. Access for remote workforces

Applications which need their applications to access third-party contractors should ensure their security technology provides a seamless remote workforce access with the ability to protect both data and systems from unauthorized access.

Also, the organization should focus on using technologies which facilitate the creation of customized business policies and rules for the remote workers.

3. Frictionless two-factor Authentication

For an organization to maintain the integrity of their system and the efficiency of their workforce, the login access should be made secure and effortless. If users are needed to go through multiple steps so as to login to a system, productivity will be reduced and users will be incentivized to find ways of bypassing the security protocols.

A good context-based authentication solution is the one which provides a frictionless and multi-factor authentication capable of passively assessing the trustworthiness of the attempted logins.

4. Shared global intelligence

With shared intelligence, the value of context-based authentication can be increased by combining the multi-factor authentication with real-time data network of known, global security threats.

Exploits

The context-based authentication can be exploited, which is a threat to cybersecurity. The following are some of the exploits which can be performed on context-based authentication:

1. Impersonation

This occurs when a malicious user uses a system by login using the credentials of another legitimate user. The malicious will have all the rights and privileges of a legitimate user, which is a great threat to cyber-security. Users should take care of their account credentials so that they are not revealed to any other individuals. Impersonation can also be thwarted by use of a multi-factor authentication mechanism.

2. Session hijack

A session is the period between the login and logout of an account. If you are accessing a website, a malicious can hijack the session by placing himself between your computer and the web server as you are engaged in active session.

The malicious user is able to see anything you do on your account, and they are capable of kicking you out so as to exercise full control of your account. The malicious attacker is capable of accessing and even modifying the server information without having to hack a registered account.

To thwart this kind of attack, a long and random number should be used as the session key. The data between the communicating parties also need to be encrypted. The session id should also be regenerated after a successful login.

3. Man in the Middle attack

This is a kind of attack in which a communication between two systems is intercepted. The malicious attacker hijacks the communication between the two communicating parties, impersonates both parties and gains access to the information the two parties are trying to send to each other.

To prevent this type of attack, verification and encryption methods should be used. Users should avoid WIFI networks which are not protected by passwords. If a secure application is not in use, you should log out immediately.

4. Cross site scripting

This is abbreviated as XSS and it is a common vulnerability in most web applications. It allows an attacker to inject content into a website and change how it is rendered. The browser of the victim is forced to execute the attacker's code when the page is being loaded.

XSS vulnerabilities expect to be triggered by the users by waiting for someone to visit a webpage or via social engineering. To prevent this, output encoding should be done based on context.

5. Privilege Escalation
This type of attack occurs when a particular user gets access to extra functionalities or resources that they are not supposed to access. The logged in user or application ends up doing actions that they are not intended to by the administrator.

The degree to which escalation is done depends on the privileges one can obtain after a successful exploit.
Vertical escalation occurs when one is able to access resources which are only accessible to accounts with more privileges. Horizontal escalation occurs when one accesses resources which are granted to accounts with a similar configuration.

Conclusion

This marks the end of this book. We have discussed the topics which are tested in the CompTIA CSA+ exam. Organizations should be prepared enough to ensure that their computer systems are safe from cyber-attacks. They should monitor their systems continuously as a way of detecting any possible or potential attacks. They should also assess their systems so as to identify any vulnerability. These should be handled before a cyber-attack can occur. Organizations should have cybersecurity professionals, who should be tasked with the responsibility of ensuring the organization is safe from cyber-attacks. A plan should be created which will be followed in case of occurrence of a cyber-attack. Every member in the organization should be made aware of this plan. Organizations should also be well prepared so as to collect evidence by use of forensic tools in case an attack occurs.

www.ingramcontent.com/pod-product-compliance
Lightning Source LLC
LaVergne TN
LVHW052316060326
832902LV00021B/3926